W9-AGB-107

DILEMMAS IN

DEMOCRACY

Money in Politics

Derek Miller

Cavendish
Square

New York

Published in 2020 by Cavendish Square Publishing, LLC
243 5th Avenue, Suite 136, New York, NY 10016

Library of Congress Cataloging-in-Publication Data

Names: Miller, Derek L., author.
Title: Money in politics / Derek Miller.
Description: First edition. | New York : Cavendish Square, 2020. | Series:
Dilemmas in democracy | Audience: Grades 7-12. | Includes bibliographical references and index.
Identifiers: LCCN 2018056809 (print) | LCCN 2019000320 (ebook) |
ISBN 9781502644947 (ebook) | ISBN 9781502644930 (library bound) | ISBN 9781502644923 (pbk.)
Subjects: LCSH: Money--Political aspects--United States--Juvenile literature. |
Political culture--United States--Juvenile literature. | Campaign funds--
United States--Juvenile literature. | Democracy--Juvenile literature.
Classification: LCC JK1991 (ebook) | LCC JK1991 .M63 2020 (print) | DDC 324.7/80973--dc23
LC record available at https://lccn.loc.gov/2018056809

Editorial Director: David McNamara
Editor: Caitlyn Miller
Copy Editor: Alex Tessman
Associate Art Director: Alan Sliwinski
Designer: Christina Shults
Production Coordinator: Karol Szymczuk
Photo Research: J8 Media

The photographs in this book are used by permission and through the courtesy of:
Cover fStop Images/Antenna/Getty Images; background (and used throughout the book) Artist
Elizaveta/Shutterstock.com; p. 4 Chip Somodevilla/Getty Images; p. 7 Frank Polich/Getty Images; p. 13
Buffaloboy/Shutterstock.com; p. 15 Jeremy Kemp/Wikimedia Commons/File:Gerrymander diagram
for four sample districts.gif/Public Domain; p. 17 Alex Wong/Getty Images; p. 21 Milosluz/iStock/
Getty Images; p. 22 Mark Wilson/Getty Images; p. 26 Chip Somodevilla/Getty Images; p. 30 Chip
Somodevilla/Getty Images; p. 34 Gillian Handyside, Christopher Huffaker, Jean-Michel Cornu/AFP/
Newscom; p. 38 Nicholas Kamm/AFP/Getty Images; p. 40 Alex Wong/Getty Images; p. 42 EQ Roy/
Shutterstock.com; p. 44 Pius Utomi Ekpei/AFP/Getty Images; p. 46 Canuckguy/Wikimedia Commons/
File:EIU Democracy Index 2017.svg/CC BY-SA 4.0; p. 49 Phil Walter/Getty Images; p. 52 Vince Talotta/
Toronto Star/Getty Images; p. 55 Jung Yeon-Je/AFP/Getty Images; p. 56 Jordan Krueger/TNS/Newscom;
p. 59 David Paul Morris/Bloomberg/Getty Images; p. 61 Manny Ceneta/AFP/Getty Images; p. 62 Tom
Williams/CQ Roll Call/AP Images; p. 66 Mark Wilson/Getty Images; p. 70 George Frey/Getty Images.

Printed in the United States of America

CONTENTS

CHAPTER 1

The Effects of Money in Politics

Money is necessary in politics. In a democracy, candidates must spend money to campaign for office. They travel the country speaking to crowds. They buy television advertisements explaining their views. Political parties have offices that they must rent and staff. All this costs money—sometimes a great deal of it.

The Problems of Money

Money in politics is not always a bad thing, but sometimes it can lead to problems. The challenge that democratic governments face is how to regulate money in politics. Different countries have different laws doing so. Laws typically govern how politicians can raise money and how much money they can spend. For instance, many countries ban politicians from accepting money from foreign governments. Accepting foreign money may influence how they act toward other countries.

Opposite: Political events like the 2016 Republican National Convention cost tens of millions of dollars.

Other issues are less clear-cut: Should politicians be able to accept unlimited money from a rich donor? Should politicians be required to publish the name of every person who gives them money? There are no easy answers to these questions. Before we look at how the American government, and other governments, have tackled these issues, we will look at the possible negative effects and current debates surrounding money in politics.

Corruption and Influence

The most obvious problem of money in politics is the possibility of corruption. Corruption is difficult to define. It can occur at very low levels, such as a police officer accepting a bribe. Corruption can also occur in the halls of power. Heads of state in countries around the world have been accused and convicted of accepting bribes in return for decisions that affected citizens.

Typically, corruption is the abuse of power for personal gain. When politicians are corrupt, they betray the public trust. Politicians oversee huge amounts of money and power. The public expects them to manage these resources effectively for the public good. They should not distribute them for their own personal gain.

Accepting a bribe is not the only kind of corruption, but it is the most straightforward example. It is illegal for politicians to accept money in return for political favors. Favors can include business contracts, like the construction of a bridge. They can also have much bigger stakes. In 2011, former Illinois governor Rod Blagojevich was convicted of corruption for trying to sell a seat in the US Senate! As governor, he had the power to appoint a replacement when Senator Barack Obama became president, vacating the seat.

Aside from Governor Blagojevich, many other politicians in the United States have been found guilty of accepting bribes in

Former Illinois governor Rod Blagojevich was convicted of corruption and sentenced to fourteen years in prison in 2011.

return for taking action on some issue. One example is former congressman Duke Cunningham. In 2005, Cunningham admitted to accepting millions of dollars in cash and gifts, including a house, a yacht, and money for a Rolls Royce. In return, he influenced how government contracts were given out. Companies that gave him money were funneled federal tax money.

Corruption allows money to influence how the government works. If politicians can be bought, rich people and businesses can influence government actions. This is a major threat to democracy.

Transparency and Public Trust

The appearance of corruption is just as worrying to lawmakers and judges as actual corruption. When citizens of a democracy believe that the government is corrupt, they stop trusting the government. They may stop voting in elections, believing that all candidates are corrupt and elections do not matter. Citizens may also stop cooperating with the police and tax collectors, seeing them as agents of a corrupt government that does not have their best interests in mind.

For this reason, democratic governments do their best to avoid even the appearance of corruption. One of the best ways to do this is through transparency. Transparency in governance means that there is openness and accountability. Information about how the government operates is publicly available. While most individuals may not review government records, they know that journalists can and do search for wrongdoing.

Accountability means that when crimes occur, someone is held responsible. In the example of Duke Cunningham, accountability led to a sentence of eight years and four months in prison. When politicians are punished for corruption, it makes it clear that such behavior is not tolerated.

Policy Capture

Corruption is related to another issue called policy capture. Policy capture is when government decisions are determined by special interests rather than the public good. In some cases, it is clearly illegal, such as when a politician accepts money in return for supporting a law. Yet in other cases, policy capture is much more complicated.

Sometimes, politicians accept campaign contributions from a group, and years later they take the side of that group in a debate. The politician likely received the campaign contribution because they were sympathetic to the group's views in the first place. There may be no clear link between the money and actions of the politician. This is not necessarily corruption. Nonetheless, it is a threat to democracy when politicians favor special interest groups over the public good.

In the United States, policy capture is often a concern when it comes to business regulation. Regulations are meant to protect the economy and individuals in a country. For example, environmental regulations are meant to protect water, soil, and air quality. These regulations force companies to spend money to clean up after their activities. Industries often lobby Congress to relax these regulations. If industries do not need to spend as much money keeping the environment clean, they can increase their profits. However, poor air and water quality harm the people living around factories. When the interests of businesses win out over the interests of ordinary people, this is policy capture. Like corruption, it can create distrust between citizens and their government.

Political Lobbies

Policy capture is closely tied to lobbying in the United States. Lobbying is attempting to influence the passage of legislation—or laws. Legislation is the foundation of the government. It is the job of congresspeople to pass, update, and repeal—or get rid of—laws. When many people think of laws, they think of the laws that determine what is or is not a crime. Yet many laws do not touch on criminal matters. Laws govern how the government functions, how programs that provide health insurance work, and the many regulations and requirements that businesses must follow.

Lobbyists are hired by clients to influence laws. Large corporations often have entire lobbying departments that work in Washington, DC. These lobbyists try to influence legislation at every level. They push for new laws that would benefit their clients, such as government subsidies, or payments, to their industry. Lobbyists seek to shape laws that are being written. They also argue for the repeal of laws that they do not like—such as regulations that cost money to follow.

One recent controversy that drew in lobbyists is food labeling. Today, genetically modified organisms (GMOs) go into a great deal of food in supermarkets. GMOs have been altered by scientists in order to change their characteristics. For instance, most corn grown in the United States is genetically modified. Scientists genetically engineered it to be resistant to an herbicide—a chemical that kills plants. The herbicide is then sprayed on the crop of corn to kill all the weeds that are not resistant to it.

Some consumer groups want GMOs to be labeled on food. Most corporations that produce food disagree. They worry that labeling will cost money, and consumers may assume a label means GMOs are harmful in some way. For years, these groups have battled over legislation on food labels. The food industry spent hundreds of millions of dollars to lobby against labeling requirements.

In 2016, legislation was finally passed that would eventually require labels on food made with GMOs. But there was a catch. Rather than a label with words, companies could opt to use a QR code—a barcode that requires you take a picture of it with a smartphone to see what it says. Consumer groups and some lawmakers complained that the QR codes would make it very difficult to tell if a food was made with GMOs. Shoppers would be forced to take pictures of labels on food packaging with their smartphone—if they owned one—in order to see if it was made with GMOs. In this case, lobbyists succeeded in shaping a law to benefit their clients as it was being written.

Lobbying is legal in the United States. Its supporters argue that companies have a right to be heard by lawmakers. They say it makes sense that the experts who work in a field can weigh in on legislation. Opponents to lobbying say that the lobbying industry is out of control. It has seen huge growth in the past few decades. Billions of dollars are now spent on lobbying each year.

Another concern is that there has been a great deal of overlap between people working in government and lobbyists. This is sometimes called the "revolving door." People go back and forth between government and lobbying jobs—taking money from corporations to lobby for changes and then working in government roles that make decisions on those very issues. In the following chapter, we will return to this issue of the revolving door. Its practice has drawn criticism from both Republicans and Democrats.

QR codes, like the one shown here on a smartphone screen, can be used for everything from labeling food to facilitating purchases. QR codes are at the center of a debate about labeling GMO foods.

Funding in Elections

Billions of dollars are spent on lobbying each year. However, this is not the only legal source of money in politics. Presidential and congressional elections cost even more money. In 2016, the Center for Responsive Politics estimated that $6.4 billion was spent on that year's US federal elections. Federal elections are for lawmakers who govern the entire country, like the president and members of Congress. They do not include state and local elections for governors and state legislators. These, too, are funded by donations, but they tend to draw far less money.

In 2016, approximately $4 billion was spent on US congressional races, while $2.4 billion was spent on the presidential election. The winner of the presidential race, Donald Trump, spent less than his opponent, Hillary Clinton. Trump's campaign spent $398 million while Clinton's campaign spent $768 million. This was notable because it was the first time since 1996 that the candidate who spent less money won the presidency.

In fact, how much money a candidate spends is very important to the outcome of a federal election. Trump's victory was a departure from the norm. Trump's supporters point to the fact that his message must have appealed to voters. His critics say that the media covered his campaign more than any other candidate's. A *mediaQuant* analysis found that Trump received $1.72 billion more than Clinton in free media coverage. This was due in part to the attention-grabbing nature of many of his remarks on camera.

There is no doubt that having more money gives a candidate an advantage in an election. It makes it possible for them to communicate with more voters through mail, television ads, and at events. People who want reform of the American system of electoral fundraising point to the fact that 95 percent of better-funded congressional candidates won. From this figure, it is not hard to see why candidates spend so much of their time fundraising. Reformers worry that candidates are forced to listen to the people who donate money to their campaign more than the citizens they represent. If who has the most money determines who wins, candidates cannot help but focus on donors and fundraising.

It is important to remember that there is more to the 95 percent figure than meets the eye. Many congressional races are one-sided. There is little doubt which party will take some seats in the House and Senate. This is due in part to gerrymandering. Gerrymandering is the drawing of districts on a map to favor one party. District lines are drawn so that certain seats are almost guaranteed to go to one party or another. Both parties know that certain neighborhoods and areas tend to vote for or against them based on data from the past.

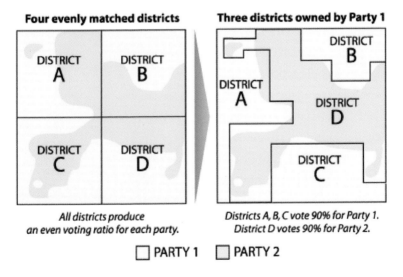

Four evenly matched districts

DISTRICT
A

DISTRICT
B

DISTRICT
C

DISTRICT
D

*All districts produce
an even voting ratio for each party.*

Three districts owned by Party 1

DISTRICT
B

DISTRICT
A

DISTRICT
D

DISTRICT
C

*Districts A, B, C vote 90% for Party 1.
District D votes 90% for Party 2.*

☐ PARTY 1   ☐ PARTY 2

This example shows how manipulating the location of voting districts can give one political party an overwhelming advantage.

Gerrymandering gives the party that draws the district lines an advantage. It also means that candidates who are almost certain to lose an election are unlikely to raise much money. This helps explain why 95 percent of better-funded candidates win. Many of them are better funded because their opponent had little chance of winning to begin with.

Silencing Views

Electoral funding can also disadvantage some candidates and views. Since politicians often rely on money from businesses and rich donors to get elected, people who oppose big businesses struggle to get elected. Even politicians representing popular opinions might fail to get elected if they oppose big businesses. Without money to run a campaign, it may not matter that a politician's views align with the views of most voters.

Winning a seat in Congress requires a great deal of fundraising.
Campaigns usually spend millions.

Securing funding can be especially problematic for female and minority candidates. In many countries around the world, female and minority candidates are incorrectly seen as less capable. This makes it more difficult for them to raise money and fund a campaign. As a result, they are underrepresented in political circles. In turn, the issues that matter to these groups may be neglected.

A related issue is that women and minority communities often earn less income in countries around the world. Candidates who express the views of women and minorities may not be able to fundraise as effectively because these groups do not have as much money to donate.

These circumstances raise concerns about fairness in democratic elections. The views of women and minority groups often go unvoiced by candidates who rely on large donations to get elected. Politicians are forced to represent businesses and rich donors to receive money and get elected. The people politicians are supposed to represent may not have their concerns addressed.

The State of the Debate Today

The question of money in American politics is very controversial. People on different sides of the issue have very strong opinions. On the one hand, people argue that money results in corruption. Donors who give millions of dollars to candidates and political parties must expect something in return. Large donations also mean that politicians need to attract rich donors and businesses for donations. Instead of focusing on ordinary Americans, they focus on fundraising from the extraordinarily wealthy.

On the other hand, defenders of money in politics believe that large donations are protected by the US Constitution. The First Amendment protects freedom of speech. Defenders of money in politics believe that the freedom of speech includes giving money to political candidates. Donations are how people show their support and help candidates they agree with. As a result, some people believe that any limits to political donations are forbidden by the Constitution.

Currently, there are many restrictions on political donations. How much an individual can give to a candidate is limited. For the elections in 2018, a person could only give $2,700 to the campaign of a candidate for the Senate or the US House of Representatives. However, someone could give $33,900 to a political party committee, such as the Republican National Committee or Democratic National Committee. These committees use some of this donated money to support political candidates. Organizations called Super PACs can also accept unlimited money from individuals and businesses. While they cannot coordinate with candidates directly, they can support them. They often run television ads in favor of a candidate or attacking an opponent.

The question of transparency is also related to this debate over money in politics and free speech. Most large donations are disclosed. This means information about them is made available to the public. When a corporation gives a large amount of money to a Super PAC, it must be reported. Voters can access this information. Typically, the media covers a controversial donation. Disclosure is meant to combat corruption. If a political party passes an unpopular law to benefit a corporation that gave them money, voters will know about the donation.

The First Amendment

The US Constitution does not weigh in on the debate concerning money in politics. There is no mention of how elections should be financed, lobbyist groups, or even political parties. Instead, laws and court cases throughout American history have resulted in today's relationship between money and politics. Nonetheless, one portion of the Constitution has played a large role in court decisions on campaign finance and lobbying:

> Congress shall make no law respecting an establishment of religion, or prohibiting the free exercise thereof; or abridging the freedom of speech, or of the press; or the right of the people peaceably to assemble, and to petition the government for a redress of grievances.

This is the First Amendment. It protects freedom of speech, the freedom of the press, the freedom to practice religion, the freedom of people to assemble—or gather in groups—and the freedom to ask the government for help. These are some of the most important freedoms that Americans enjoy.

What the Founding Fathers who wrote the First Amendment in 1791 did not know was that courts would later equate freedom of speech with donating money to campaigns. This first occurred in the 1976 Supreme Court ruling *Buckley v. Valeo*. It was reaffirmed in some of the most important court cases of modern times and resulted in the current system of campaign finance.

The US Constitution is the highest law of the land. Regulations about campaign finance and lobbying must align with the Constitution.

Supreme Court justice Clarence Thomas says the Constitution protects political donations as part of freedom of speech.

Arguments for Change

Issues of capping campaign contributions and disclosing donations are at the heart of debates about money in American politics. Right now, there are many rules and regulations that limit contributions and require the disclosure of donors. Nevertheless, many people believe these rules should be tightened. Critics think that Super PACs should not allow for unlimited contributions to causes by individuals and businesses. Additionally, it's not always clear where contributions come from. Many people believe there should be more transparency. After all, the source of money can be hidden by funneling it through different businesses and charities before donations are made.

Other Americans believe there are too many restrictions. They are in favor of getting rid of contribution limits and disclosure entirely. One of the most famous supporters of this position is Supreme Court justice Clarence Thomas. Thomas has argued that both requiring disclosure and limiting contributions are unconstitutional. He believes that freedom of speech in the First Amendment of the Constitution extends to both issues. If contributing to a campaign is protected by the First Amendment, he does not believe donations can be capped at a dollar amount.

Freedom of speech is a basic right. At the same time, Thomas believes there is a freedom to *anonymous* speech. That is why he thinks disclosure is also unconstitutional. Thomas has argued that disclosure can result in donors being harassed and threatened. Thomas's opinions are more extreme than most, but they show just how far some people believe the freedom of speech extends—and the effect of freedom of speech on money in politics.

International Institute for Democracy and Electoral Assistance

Every democracy grapples with questions surrounding money and politics. Different countries make different rules about how politicians can fundraise. Some countries allow elections to be extremely expensive affairs, while others place strict limits on spending. There is no widely accepted "best" way to handle election spending, although there are arguments for what does and does not work in individual countries. The International Institute of Democracy and Electoral Assistance (International IDEA) is an intergovernmental organization that helps countries to promote democracy and provides expert opinions on the complications of money in politics.

International IDEA is made up of thirty-one member states from around the world. It includes some of the strongest democracies, such as Norway and Sweden, as well as ones that have struggled recently with corruption and unfair elections. (The United States is not a member.)

International IDEA's mission is to "advance democracy worldwide, as a universal human aspiration and an enabler of sustainable development, through support to the building, strengthening, and safeguarding of democratic political institutions and processes at all levels." To do this, it works with governments as well as the United Nations. It also gathers data from countries around the world. This helps researchers determine what political systems are working and why.

One key area that International IDEA studies is money in politics. Its 2017 report *The Global State of Democracy: Exploring Democracy's Resilience* discusses three problems that can come from money in politics: "unequal access to funding" (for parties and candidates), "increased corruption and policy capture," and "decreased public trust in politics." All three are a threat to democracies around the world.

Unequal access to funding results in some ideas not being represented in government. If an idea has wide popular support but little funding, there may be little political will to carry it out. As a government fails to act on a popular idea, people trust the government less.

Corruption is also a major threat to people's trust in government. When politicians get wealthy through doing favors for businesses and the wealthy, people stop believing the government is there to help them. Lack of trust in government can have many terrible consequences. Citizens can stop paying their taxes, cooperating with the police, voting in elections, and abiding by laws.

In worst-case scenarios, criminal organizations such as drug traffickers can even use large sums of money to buy influence. Some commentators have used the word "narco-state" to describe this situation. When politicians rely on money from drug traffickers and criminals, the government turns a blind eye to their activities. This causes crime inside the country that often affects ordinary people. It also presents a challenge for nations around the world that seek to curb the worldwide trade in illegal drugs.

International IDEA's outreach and data collection helps confront these problems around the world. They work to limit the negative impact of money in politics and strengthen democracy. They do not take a hard stance on a best system or try to undermine the systems that democratic governments use, showing that every democracy is unique and has unique needs.

CHAPTER 2

Money in American Politics Today

The problem of money in politics is a thorny issue. In the 2016 US presidential election, Democrat Hillary Clinton and Republican Donald Trump both criticized the role of money in politics. There is widespread agreement that campaign finance laws and the current system of lobbying are not perfect. However, there is little agreement about what to do to improve the situation. Recent laws to regulate campaign finance have even come under attack by reformers for their unintended consequences. Additionally, Supreme Court rulings have struck down key parts of these laws. The current situation is quite complex, and an understanding of history is necessary to see how issues of money in politics have evolved.

Early Campaign Finance Reform

The first law to deal with campaign finance was passed in 1867. It was a law related to the Navy that also forbade political candidates from asking naval yard workers for political

Opposite: Television ads are one of the biggest expenses for political campaigns. Here, a political ad plays in an electronics store.

donations. Over the coming years, more and more laws to do with campaign finance were passed. An 1883 law forbade asking civil service employees for donations. Prior to this, government workers were expected to donate money to their parties' candidates to keep their job. (This system would be considered a clear-cut example of corruption today.)

A flurry of laws in the first half of the 1900s tried to regulate campaign finance. They limited how much people could donate to campaigns, how much campaigns could spend, and prevented corporations from giving money to federal campaigns. However, these efforts were not effectively enforced.

It was only in 1971 that the current system of campaign finance began with the passage of the Federal Election Campaign Act (FECA). The act was amended several times during the 1970s, and the Federal Election Commission (FEC), a government agency, was set up to enforce campaign finance laws.

The strict rules of FECA were challenged by a group of politicians, resulting in the important Supreme Court decision *Buckley v. Valeo*. In this decision, the court ruled that limits on individual contributions to a campaign were constitutional. This was a critical win for supporters of campaign finance regulation. However, the court ruled three key provisions unconstitutional. It struck down limits on total spending by campaigns, limits on candidates spending their own money, and limits on independent expenditures. (Independent expenditures are money spent by an outside group on a candidate's behalf.) Importantly, *Buckley v. Valeo* also equated money with free speech. This set the stage for future court decisions.

The Lead-Up to *Citizens United*

Although weakened by *Buckley v. Valeo*, the Federal Election Campaign Act continued to regulate campaign finance. Eventually, political parties began to take advantage of loopholes in the law. This led to the use of "soft money" in the 1990s. Soft money was money given to a political party—such as the Republican or Democratic Party. It was not capped like donations to campaigns because it was illegal for parties to use this money to help individual candidates. However, both the Republican and Democratic Parties began using a loophole to avoid this issue. They ran attack ads against their opponents paid for by soft money. While not technically illegal, it let parties use unlimited soft money to influence elections in a roundabout way.

In 2002, Congress passed the Bipartisan Campaign Reform Act (BCRA) to close this loophole and regulate soft money. This law is also commonly called the McCain-Feingold Act after the two senators who championed it. BCRA got rid the of the soft money that political parties had used to channel unlimited donations into races. Now campaigns were funded only by individual contributions, and these contributions were capped.

One key part of BCRA was banning corporations and labor unions from running political ads within sixty days of a general election or thirty days of a primary election. Labor unions are organizations of workers. Their political power used to rival that of corporations, but today they do not control nearly as much money as corporations.

BCRA's restriction on corporate money was challenged in the courts. It survived early challenges, but this changed in 2010.

Decisions by the nine justices of the Supreme Court have shaped campaign finance laws.

The Supreme Court decision *Citizens United v. FEC* struck down the ban on ads paid for by corporations and labor unions. It was a close decision. Five justices formed a narrow majority, while four justices disagreed. The majority opinion was that the BCRA restriction violated the freedom of speech of corporations. The majority opinion looked back to the *Buckley v. Valeo* decision that had found money and speech to be one and the same.

PACs and Super PACs

Citizens United means that corporations can spend unlimited money trying to get candidates elected. However, they still cannot directly contribute to campaigns. Instead, they can buy ads supporting a candidate or attacking an opponent at election time. They are forbidden from coordinating with the candidates or their campaigns directly.

Citizens United and later court decisions based on it laid the groundwork for Super PACs. ("PAC" stands for "political action committee.") Super PACs are organizations that accept donations and then spend the money to help candidates they support. Super PACs are the way that unlimited corporate and individual money is used to influence elections. Unlike donations to candidates and parties, there is no limit to how much a person can give a Super PAC. The largest Super PACs raise tens of millions of dollars in an election cycle.

Super PACs are regulated by the Federal Election Commission. Super PACs must disclose their donors to the FEC, even though their donations are not capped in any way. The FEC also makes sure that Super PACs do not coordinate with candidates or their campaigns.

In addition to Super PACs, there are also PACs. PACs are quite different. They can contribute money directly to candidates and campaigns. As a result, contributions to PACs are subject to the same limits as contributions to campaigns. The PACs themselves are also limited in how much they can give a single candidate. PACs tend to be less controversial than Super PACs since they are subject to caps on donations and spending.

Campaign Finance Today

Citizens United resulted in the current state of campaign finance in the United States. Corporations and labor unions can give unlimited money to Super PACs. Super PACs may try to influence elections by running ads at any time. Their one major restriction is they must remain independent and not coordinate with campaigns.

Individuals can give money to candidates, political parties, PACs, Super PACs, and other less influential organizations. The amount that an individual could donate in a single election cycle used to have a cap. Then, in 2014, the Supreme Court declared this cap unconstitutional. The *McCutcheon v. FEC* ruling once again equated money with free speech. It found that contributions by an individual to a single candidate could be capped. However, it said an individual was free to give money up to the limit to any number of candidates, parties, and PACs.

As a result, rich individuals and corporations can give huge sums of money in an election cycle. According to the Center for Responsive Politics, the largest individual donor in the 2016 election cycle was Sheldon Adelson. He gave more than $87 million to Republican candidates, PACs, Super PACs, and the Republican Party. Adelson was not alone in spending an extraordinary amount of money on the election. The top one hundred individual donors all gave more than a million dollars. Almost all of them supported just one party and its candidates.

Funding the US presidential candidates

Money raised by the different types of group supporting the election candidates

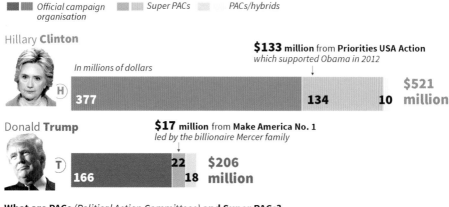

Official campaign organisation Super PACs PACs/hybrids

Hillary **Clinton**

In millions of dollars

$133 million from **Priorities USA Action**
which supported Obama in 2012

377 134 10

$521 million

Donald **Trump**

$17 million from **Make America No. 1**
led by the billionaire Mercer family

166 22 18

$206 million

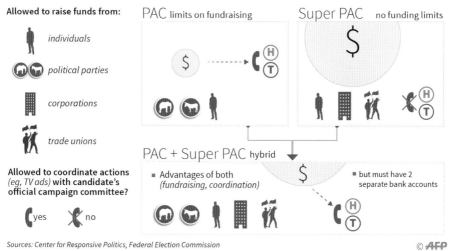

What are PACs *(Political Action Committees)* **and Super PACs?**

Allowed to raise funds from:

PAC limits on fundraising   Super PAC no funding limits

- individuals
- political parties
- corporations
- trade unions

PAC + Super PAC hybrid

- Advantages of both
  (fundraising, coordination)
- but must have 2 separate bank accounts

Allowed to coordinate actions *(eg, TV ads)* **with candidate's official campaign committee?**

yes no

Sources: Center for Responsive Politics, Federal Election Commission   © AFP

Hillary Clinton received far more support from Super PACs than Donald Trump did during the 2016 presidential campaign cycle.

Current Debates

Recent Supreme Court decisions like *Citizens United* have been incredibly important. Never before has freedom of speech been so closely tied to the right to donate unlimited money to influence elections. In the Supreme Court's opinion, Super PACs do not lead to corruption or the appearance of corruption because they are independent. They do not communicate with campaigns. However, many Americans disagree. They worry that unlimited corporate money will lead to corruption. A 2012 *Washington Post*-ABC News poll found that 69 percent of voters wanted Super PACs to be illegal.

The Revolving Door

Another issue that causes controversy in the United States today is the so-called revolving door. This phrase refers to the practice of lobbyists going to work for the government and former government officials becoming lobbyists. People spend their careers bouncing between the two positions. They accept money from corporations to lobby for changes to federal regulations and then take jobs to enforce the very regulations they were paid to change. In the worst cases, critics claim it amounts to industries writing and enforcing the regulations meant to prevent those industries from doing harm.

The revolving door has proved difficult to close. In 2007, Barack Obama made closing the revolving door a central platform of his presidential campaign. Harnessing negative feelings toward lobbyists and politicians, he promised that if he were elected president, things would change. After he took office, he made some headway on the issue, although dozens of former lobbyists joined his administration. Obama issued an executive order—one of the most powerful tools of the president—forbidding government officials who left their job from lobbying their former government coworkers for two years.

President Trump continued these efforts. As a candidate, he promised to "drain the swamp" of Washington, DC, putting an end to apparent corruption and close ties between lobbyists and government. He, too, signed an executive order that tried to shut the revolving door. It banned former lobbyists who took jobs in the government from working on matters related to the companies they lobbied for within the past two years. However, the White House reserved the right to issue waivers on this issue. Many government officials have received these waivers. The waivers allow them to work on issues that relate to companies that recently paid them large sums of money.

It is helpful to look at examples of the revolving door. As of early 2018, about one-third of the people that President Trump appointed to the Environmental Protection Agency (EPA) had formerly been lobbyists for companies like chemical manufacturers and fossil fuel producers. These are the companies that the EPA is supposed to police, ensuring that they follow tight regulations to protect the environment. In other words, many of these people in the EPA had previously lobbied against the very regulations they were now supposed to enforce.

One notable example Andrew Wheeler, who began serving as head of the EPA in July 2018. Wheeler is a former lobbyist for the energy industry. His lobbying company received millions of dollars from many clients, including Murray Energy. Murray Energy has a long history of legal battles with the EPA over whether the company follows regulations. As head of the EPA, Wheeler will be in charge of the EPA in any future conflicts with Murray Energy, his former client. Additionally, Wheeler will be responsible for enforcing regulations that he worked to repeal as a lobbyist. For example, as a lobbyist, he worked to repeal a current rule that forbids coal companies from dumping waste into streams.

The revolving door results in many conflicts of interest like this. Wheeler's position is not unique. Many former lobbyists work in the government. This places them in a difficult position where they must take on former employers and clients. Their position is especially difficult since they will leave the government one day—and likely try to get a job in the same industry they are supposed to police.

Gifts in Politics

Despite the revolving door, there are many restrictions on lobbyists and lawmakers at the federal level. One of the most important is a ban on gifts to lawmakers by lobbyists. This includes not only obvious gifts like giving money to lawmakers, but also less obvious offerings, like buying them meals. House ethics rules spell out that even free rounds of golf count as a gift.

At the state level, restrictions of gifts vary. Some states follow strict guidelines like those at the federal level. Other states do not. This invites accusations of corruption. In Pennsylvania, cash gifts from lobbyists to lawmakers were only banned in 2014 after a scandal. However, other kinds of gifts, like vacations and hotel bookings, are still legal.

Cases of politicians accepting gifts have been quite common in recent years. One important case was that of former Virginia governor Bob McDonnell. During his time as governor, McDonnell accepted at least $175,000 worth of gifts from a businessman. In return, he arranged meetings on the businessman's behalf and appeared at events with him, helping him to make business deals.

The US Chamber of Commerce

Every year, billions of dollars are spent lobbying for political change in Washington, DC. This money gives the largest lobbies a great deal of influence in politics. Politicians know that if they support a lobbying group, their campaign can receive money. If they oppose it, they may be subject to attack ads, and their rivals may see more funding.

One of the most important lobbying groups is the US Chamber of Commerce. Despite its name, it is not affiliated with the government

Secretary of State Mike Pompeo speaks at an event hosted by the US Chamber of Commerce.

in any way. It is a lobbying group that supports pro-business policies. In 2016, the US Chamber of Commerce reported that it spent $103,950,000 dollars on its lobbying efforts. According to the Center of Responsive Politics, $10 million was spent in support of Republican candidates, and just under $2 million was spent attacking Democratic and Republican candidates. No money was spent supporting Democratic candidates.

In addition to election funding, the US Chamber of Commerce tries to influence policy. It supports pro-business measures, such as favorable trade deals with other countries. It tries to block bills it sees as anti-business. Controversially, it has opposed legislation meant to slow global climate change as well as many other environmental laws. In 2009, its position on climate change led Apple to quit the US Chamber of Commerce. Like all lobbying groups with many backers, the US Chamber of Commerce struggles to please all its donors.

Former Virginia governor Bob McDonnell was convicted of corruption in 2014, but the Supreme Court overturned the conviction.

McDonnell was later convicted of corruption and sentenced to two years in prison.

In 2016, the Supreme Court overturned McDonnell's conviction. The court ruled that acts like arranging meetings and private events did not rise to the level of corruption. They ruled McDonnell's actions were not official government acts, like casting a vote or awarding a government contract are. Critics were outraged by the Supreme Court decision. They argue it makes it legal for some government officials to use their political position to receive money in return for favors—so long as they take no official government action. Other corruption convictions have been overturned based on the Supreme Court ruling.

Nearly all Americans oppose politicians receiving gifts in return for favors. McDonnell himself admitted that he had made mistakes, although he did not believe he had acted criminally. However, opinions differ on how best to tackle this issue. The Supreme Court argued that something like arranging a meeting was too routine of an act to be criminal—even if a politician received a gift for it. People who want reform think that the current laws about corruption need to be tightened, especially in states with looser rules. There is little doubt that cases like McDonnell's lead to the appearance of corruption and further mistrust of politicians.

Foreign Influences

Al Jazeera is headquartered in Doha, Qatar. There is much debate about foreign media's influence on US policy.

It is illegal for political candidates to accept money from foreign governments. This is meant to limit the influence of foreign governments in American politics and ensure politicians are not indebted to them. Nonetheless, there are still ways that foreign governments use their money and power to try to influence American politics.

One legal way that foreign governments influence the United States is through news organizations. Media outlets like RT, funded by Russia, and Al Jazeera, funded by Qatar, broadcast in the United States. Critics say their media coverage reflects the views of the governments that fund them. On the other hand, outlets like Al Jazeera also have many supporters who say their coverage is fair even though it is different from Western media coverage.

Tariffs are another legal means that countries use to try to influence America. Tariffs are taxes on goods from another country. When President Trump announced tariffs on European and Chinese goods, affected countries responded with political pressure against Trump himself. This took the form of targeted tariffs on goods from important swing states. Swing states, like Florida, tend to decide presidential elections. As a result, tariffs targeted goods from these states like orange juice, a staple of Florida's economy, with the intent of hurting the state's economy. This was meant to hurt Trump's popularity in Florida—and convince him to lift his tariffs.

Foreign governments can also meddle in American politics in illegal ways. Russian interference in the 2016 US presidential election is an example of this. American intelligence agencies say that there was a coordinated attempt to harm Hillary Clinton's campaign and benefit her opponents Donald Trump and Bernie Sanders. This took the form of cyberattacks against Clinton and the leaking of illegally acquired emails and documents. It also included thousands of fake social media accounts—so-called trolls—that criticized Clinton and praised her opponents.

In this way, Russia spent money to hurt Clinton's chances and, according to the FBI, to "undermine public faith in the US democratic process." Russia has undertaken similar efforts in other democratic elections around the world.

CHAPTER 3

Comparing Democracies Around the World

The United States is unique in how much it spends on elections—far more than any other country. Countries around the world have very different ways of handling money in politics. No two systems are the same. In their own ways, countries hope to minimize the negative impacts of money in politics by limiting corruption and strengthening public trust in politicians.

Public Funding of Campaigns

One common way to pay for election campaigns is through public funding. Public funding is when political campaigns are given money by the government. Almost all democracies have some sort of public funding. Usually it is a mixed system where candidates get some public funding and receive some private donations. The amount of public funding is often based on the number of votes or private donations a candidate (or party) receives. Countries including Norway, Sweden, and

Opposite: Campaign posters line the streets of Accra, Ghana, in 2016.

The Democracy Index rates countries according to the strength of their democratic institutions. Dark green is used for the most democratic countries, while dark red is used for the least democratic countries.

Australia are just a few examples of democracies that use some degree of public funding for campaigns.

The United States has a system of public funding for presidential races, but it is rarely used today. Candidates can choose to opt in and receive some money from the government. However, this money comes with numerous restrictions. In the twenty-first century, few candidates have accepted public funding because of the limitations. Many reformers of campaign finance in the United States want to change the system so that more candidates choose to use public funding.

Public funding has benefits and drawbacks. In theory, it can combat some of the negative effects of money in politics. For

Money and Mistrust

A Pew Research Center report from May 2018 asked Americans how well this statement described the United States: "People who give a lot of money to elected officials *do not* have more influence than others." Just 11 percent of Americans thought that this described the country "very well," and 15 percent said it described the country "somewhat well." The rest, 74 percent of Americans, thought it described the country "not too well" or "not well at all." This reveals a shocking lack of trust in the current system of money in politics. The idea that every individual has the same influence in a democracy is its foundation. One person has one vote. When money can buy additional influence, it is a problem. When citizens believe this to be the case—rightly or wrongly—it leads to mistrust of the entire system.

In fact, the United States is exceptional with regards to how little its people trust politicians. Typically, the less corrupt a country is, the more its people trust the government. But in the United States, people report trusting politicians far less than usual for a country with so little corruption.

An International IDEA report uses numbers and polls to examine how corruption and trust relate in countries around the world. Finland and the United States are two democracies with about the same level of corruption: very little. But on a scale from 1 to 7, Finns report they trust their politicians at about a 5.7, while Americans score their trust at just 3.4. This places American trust in their politicians at about the middle of the pack—far lower than it should be considering how little corruption there is in the United States compared to many other countries.

example, public funding can help political candidates who represent the issues of marginalized groups. Marginalized groups are those that are not prioritized by society or the government. They include minority groups and women in some countries. Even mainstream candidates who represent marginalized groups may struggle to get funding. Public funding can help them get the money to fight for increased rights.

On the other hand, public funding is often tied to performance in past elections. Parties that did well in the last election receive the most money. This can be a huge benefit for parties that are already in power. In this system, public funding can help maintain the current political parties in power. It can be difficult to effect political change. New political parties do not receive much funding, if any, because they are new. Candidates who represent marginalized groups in this system may not be able to break onto the political scene in the first place.

Supporters of public funding hope that it will limit the influence of money in politics. If candidates do not have to seek money from rich donors and corporations, they will not owe them anything when the election is over. In fact, there is a connection between public funding and corruption. Countries with public funding tend to be less corrupt, but only a little.

Capping Campaign Spending

Public spending ties into another major issue of campaign finance: the total amount spent on a campaign. One of the biggest drawbacks of public funding is that it requires spending by the government. The government must raise the funds to give campaigns. This means it must use tax dollars. In other words, public funding means the taxpayers pay for an election. In a country like the United States,

In New Zealand, candidates buy inexpensive ads, like billboards, instead of numerous (expensive) television commercials.

this is a huge expense. Few taxpayers would be happy paying for the many television ads that run repeatedly during election cycles. For this reason, public funding would likely require stricter caps on spending.

In the United States, campaign finance regulations focus on how much an individual can donate to a campaign. Other countries sometimes approach this issue the opposite way. Rather than focus on individual donations, they restrict the total spending of campaigns. For instance, in New Zealand, candidates for Parliament could spend just $26,200 New Zealand dollars (less than $20,000 US) on advertising in the three months before the 2017 elections. While individual donations are not capped in New Zealand, there is little point in candidates raising huge sums of money because of this restriction on spending. Supporters for this kind of system argue that this means rich donors cannot influence politicians as easily since their money is not helpful.

Limiting the total spending of campaigns is not allowed in the United States. The Supreme Court found it unconstitutional in *Buckley v. Valeo* in 1976. Unless the Supreme Court reverses this decision or there is a constitutional amendment, campaign finance reform in the United States must focus on other issues.

Television Ads

Rather than limit campaign donations or spending, some countries take aim at television ads. Ads tend to be one of the largest expenses for campaigns. In the United States, ads are targeted at key battleground states, where a small number of votes can decide the next president. They are also a favorite way for Super PACs to spend large sums of money to try to influence the outcome of an election.

Other countries do not allow the huge number of television ads that mark an American election. Some countries require that all political parties or candidates in a race receive the same amount of airtime. If a channel runs an ad for one candidate, it must give the opponent equal time. Canada focuses on equitable (fair and impartial) airtime. In Canada, if a candidate buys airtime, their opponent must be offered the chance to buy airtime. In some nations, ads are even restricted to television channels run by the government. This makes it easy to give all candidates the same amount of limited airtime.

At the same time, television ads are a case where it is easy to see the argument that money equates to free speech. Buying a television ad is a straightforward way to tell voters about your opinion or ideas.

Public funding, restrictions on campaign spending, and limits on television ads are all ways that different countries shape their elections. They try to balance the concerns of fairness and corruption with freedom of speech.

George Smitherman, a candidate in the 2016 Toronto mayoral race, films a promo to air on TV. His opponents were offered the same opportunity by the television network.

Holding Presidents Accountable

No American president has ever been tried and convicted of crimes committed in office. There is no doubt President Richard Nixon committed crimes during the Watergate scandal, but he was pardoned after he resigned from the presidency in 1974. (Watergate involved breaking into campaign offices and destroying evidence.) As a result of the pardon, Nixon never faced punishment for his crimes. The exact nature of his crimes will never fully be known.

Critics say that Nixon should have faced criminal proceedings. President Gerald Ford justified his decision to issue a pardon on the grounds the country needed to move forward. Nonetheless, it was a serious blow to the ideals of government transparency and accountability. Ford failed to get reelected, and many commentators thought it was due in part to the pardon.

Other countries have held their leaders to stricter standards. In 2016, evidence emerged of government corruption in South Korea, a wealthy democracy. President Park Geun-hye was implicated in accepting bribes and extorting money. Later that year, she was impeached by the country's legislature. In the end, she was found guilty of numerous charges relating to misuse of money in politics. She accepted bribes in return for favors and forced companies to donate money to charities she was involved with. The case also involved the massive Korean company Samsung. The son of Samsung's chairman was sentenced to prison for paying bribes.

Park received a sentence of twenty-five years in prison for her crimes. Unlike Nixon, she was held accountable. Her sentence sends a clear message that political corruption will not be tolerated in South Korea.

Former Korean president Park Geun-hye arrives in court during her 2017 trial.

I SEE CORRUPT PEOPLE
STAND WITH MONTANA
THE PEOPLE SEE
Common Cause
Common Cause
I AM A PERSON
CORPORATIONS ARE NOT
I AM A PERSON
I WANT YOU TO
Overturn Citizens United

CHAPTER 4

The Power of the People

There are many ways for concerned citizens to weigh in on how their government is run. Despite the negative effects of money in politics, politicians answer to their voters. When the people who elect them into office make it clear that they feel strongly about an issue, politicians often listen. From protests to making phone calls, we will look at the many ways ordinary people can get involved.

Helping a Campaign

Money is not the only factor in a politician's campaign. Politicians also need volunteers to make phone calls, organize supporters, and help voters register. If you are concerned about money in politics, you can support the campaign of a candidate who shares your views. That said, it is necessary to look at the claims of politicians critically. Most politicians say they do not like the current system, but many still vote against reform

Opposite: Court decisions about campaign finance have frequently led to protests.

Volunteers for Hillary Clinton's 2016 presidential campaign make phone calls to encourage others to vote for Clinton.

efforts. However, some candidates have a proven track record of supporting change.

You can also donate money to a candidate's campaign directly. Despite the large amount of money from Super PACs, candidates still rely quite heavily on small donations. In the 2016 presidential elections, Donald Trump's campaign received 26 percent of its money from individual donations of less than $200. Hillary Clinton's campaign received 16 percent. Some other candidates received even more. Bernie Sanders, who challenged Clinton for the Democratic nomination, received 57 percent of his campaign funds from small donations.

All three of these candidates proposed some changes in the way that money influences politics. It is up to you to decide who you agree with and how likely you think it is that a candidate will carry out their ideas. Helping candidates who want to change the influence of money on politics is one of the most important ways that citizens can make a difference.

Lobbying for Change

If the current system of money in politics changes, it will likely be due to legislation. There have been many attempts to pass campaign finance bills since the McCain-Feingold Act of 2002. Between 2010 and 2018, the DISCLOSE Act has been introduced to Congress repeatedly. So far, it has failed to pass because it has not secured a majority of votes in Congress.

DISCLOSE stands for Democracy Is Strengthened by Casting Light on Spending in Elections. The DISCLOSE Act seeks to improve transparency in campaign finance. It would require Super PACs to disclose donors promptly and stop the use of common methods to hide the source of donations. The act would also require television

Republican John McCain (*left*) and Democrat Russ Feingold (*right*) co-sponsored a campaign finance bill that became law in 2002.

The Federal Election Commission

Federal campaign finance laws are enforced by the Federal Election Commission (FEC). The FEC is an independent regulatory agency with six commissioners. These commissioners are tasked with making enforcement decisions. Since the agency is independent, no more than three commissioners can belong to the same political party, and four commissioners must agree on important decisions.

The work of the FEC is important for enforcing campaign finance law. However, the agency does come under fire from politicians and the public. It had been accused of being partisan—supporting one political party over another. Votes sometimes occur along party lines, with the three Democrats and three

Members of the Federal Election Commission meet in their Washington, DC, office.

Republicans on opposite sides. This results in deadlock since four votes are required.

The FEC's important work of enforcing campaign finance laws is affected by these political issues. Some critics have even questioned why FEC commissioners are appointed by the president and Senate—the very people whose campaigns the FEC is supposed to police.

In early 2018, another problem began to cause issues at the FEC. As commissioners left, replacements were not being appointed by politicians. As of October 15, 2018, the FEC is down to just four commissioners. This means they must unanimously agree on any decision. The work of the FEC is in danger of further gridlock.

ads funded by Super PACs to reveal their top donors. This would mirror the current requirement that candidates state something to the effect of, "I approve this message," on their own ads.

Unfortunately, campaign finance reform has become a partisan issue since the bipartisan passage of the McCain-Feingold Act. Republican lawmakers oppose the DISCLOSE Act as a Democratic effort. As of late 2018, they have not responded with their own bill to regulate money in politics.

If you support the DISCLOSE Act—or a future attempt to reform campaign finance and improve transparency—you can lobby your representatives in Congress to pass it. Until this point, we have focused on lobbyist groups. Yet individuals also have the power to lobby—or try to shape the legislative process. People can call or write letters to their representative in the House and Senate. If enough people express their support of a bill, it may sway votes in Congress.

Peaceful Protest

Another way to make your voice heard is through your right to peacefully assemble. In much the same way as lobbying a lawmaker does, protests can make Congress aware of what matters to ordinary people.

A recent protest about money in politics was in 2016. The Democracy Spring organization marched from Philadelphia to Washington, DC. Once there, they sat on the steps of the US Capitol—where Congress meets—in an act of civil disobedience. Civil disobedience is a peaceful refusal to follow a law. More than one thousand protesters were arrested for sitting in the area and refusing to move. Democracy Spring did this to further their

Staying Informed

The issue of campaign finance in the United States changes quite rapidly. Court cases like *Citizens United* can alter the rules overnight. Congress often debates passing new campaign finance laws, although it has not succeeded in recent years. It is important to stay informed about ongoing changes.

Websites are a great resource for learning about current issues. Many reputable websites are devoted to the issue of campaign finance reform. For some, this is their only topic. Other times, it is one issue of many that they cover. When reading a website, it is important to look at who is behind it. Try to find websites by trusted sources. One well-respected charity organization with web pages about money in politics is the American Civil Liberties Union (ACLU).

The ACLU supports the expansion of public funding in campaign finance reform. Although public funding exists in the United States, its details mean that nearly all presidential candidates decline to take it. It is important to keep in mind the bias that sources have when looking at them. The ACLU is open about their support for public funding. Some sources do not state their potential biases so openly.

The ACLU page that deals with campaign finance reform is: https://www.aclu.org/issues/free-speech/campaign-finance-reform. It spells out their position on the matter. At the bottom, it links to recent articles that cover the topic, analyze legislation being debated in Congress, and discuss court cases. Articles like these are a valuable tool for staying informed.

Democracy Spring protesters march in Washington, DC, on April 11, 2016, to show support for campaign finance reform.

mission of "ending the corruption of big money in politics and protecting the right to vote for all people."

Protesting does not need to involve civil disobedience or breaking the law. It can simply be marching and carrying signs. The important thing is to make your opinions known. Democracy Spring supports many of the same campaign finance ideas that have been debated in Congress.

One of Democracy Spring's proposed fixes to the current system is having the government match small donations by a ratio of 6:1 or 9:1 to increase their impact. Such a system would encourage politicians to seek the favor of citizens rather than focusing on big donors. It would also encourage citizens to engage more with elections.

Moving Forward

The debate about money in politics often breaks down in partisan fighting today. Questions about free speech, the right of corporations to donate unlimited money, and the power of lobbying groups are highly controversial. People who genuinely care about the United States and its future can have very different opinions.

In such heated debates, it's good to remember that people do agree on many of these issues. By and large, politicians, the people, and the courts agree that transparency in campaign finance is a good thing. While they may disagree over the best way to have transparency, everyone wants to avoid the appearance of corruption.

According to a 2018 Pew Research Poll, 77 percent of Americans also agree that donations by individuals and groups to campaigns should be limited. The debate is over the details of the limitations and how they should be enforced. There is a great deal of agreement among Americans and politicians when it comes to money in politics.

It's the job of people in the United States to work together to find common ground and change the parts of the system that they disagree with. Lobbying your lawmaker, helping politicians you agree with get elected, and peacefully protesting are all ways that you can do this. The negative effects of money on politics can be managed if people stay involved and work to improve the system.

Voting is just one way to show how you feel about issues surrounding money in politics. You can also volunteer for campaigns, join protests, and write to Congress. Make your voice heard!

GLOSSARY

bias Prejudice or partisan slant.

bipartisan Supported by both Democrats and Republicans.

campaign finance The money that is used to run political campaigns. "Campaign finance reform" refers to attempts to change how this money is regulated.

conviction A guilty verdict in a criminal case.

electoral Relating to elections.

expenditure The spending of money.

extort To get something through threats or force.

federal Relating to the national government based in Washington, DC, rather than individual state governments.

general election The final election that selects a winner. It takes place after the primary elections that select candidates from each major political party in the United States.

impeach To formally charge a government official with a crime. Typically, this is done by the legislature, although the details vary by country.

independent expenditure Spending by groups outside of a candidate's campaign that is meant to influence an election.

lobby To try to change or shape laws.

partisan Divided by political party; supporting one political party over another.

policy capture When government decisions are determined by special interests.

primary election The elections that select one candidate from each party. Primary elections occur before the general election that selects the ultimate winner.

reform To make changes to a law or system in an effort to improve it.

regulate To make and enforce rules about something.

revolving door The practice of lobbyists finding employment in the government and government employees leaving their posts to become lobbyists .

unconstitutional Not in line with the constitution; when a court declares something unconstitutional, it is no longer allowed.

FURTHER INFORMATION

Books

Haugen, David M., and Susan Musser. *Campaign Finance.* New York: Greenhaven Publishing, 2010.

Machajewski, Sarah. *Political Corruption and the Abuse of Power.* New York: Greenhaven Publishing, 2010.

Websites

Citizens United v. FEC

https://www.history.com/topics/united-states-constitution/citizens-united

The History Channel describes the circumstances that led to *Citizens United* and the creation of Super PACs.

Contribution Limits

https://www.fec.gov/help-candidates-and-committees/candidate-taking-receipts/contribution-limits/

The FEC outlines the current limits on campaign contributions that an individual can make.

Lobbying: Top Industries

https://www.opensecrets.org/lobby/top.php

The Center for Responsive Politics breaks down how much money lobbyists have spent in the United States and who their donors are.

Videos

Campaign Finance

https://www.khanacademy.org/humanities/
ap-us-government-and-politics/political-participation/
campaign-finance/v/campaign-finance

Khan Academy explains the basics of campaign finance in the United States with helpful graphics.

Political Campaigns: Crash Course Government and Politics #39

https://www.youtube.com/watch?v=2A5QlpAyKSQ

Crash Course Government and Politics looks at how political campaigns are run in the United States and how money influences them.

BIBLIOGRAPHY

Drutman, Lee. "More Campaign Spending from More People."
Atlantic, February 15, 2015. https://www.theatlantic.com/
politics/archive/2015/02/campaign-finance-reform/385478.

Falguera, Elin, Samuel Jones, and Magnus Ohman, eds. *Funding
of Political Parties and Election Campaigns: A Handbook on
Political Finance*. Stockholm, Sweden: International IDEA,
2014.

Garrett, Sam. "The State of Campaign Finance Policy: Recent
Developments and Issues for Congress." Congressional
Research Service, June 23, 2016. https://fas.org/sgp/crs/
misc/R41542.pdf.

Gerstein, Josh. "How Obama Failed to Shut Washington's
Revolving Door." *Politico*, December 31, 2015. https://www.
politico.com/story/2015/12/barack-obama-revolving-door-
lobbying-217042.

Harris, Mary. "A Media Post-Mortem on the 2016 Presidential
Election." *mediaQuant*, November 14, 2016. https://www.
mediaquant.net/2016/11/a-media-post-mortem-on-the-
2016-presidential-election.

Lavush, Rush. "Regulation of Campaign Finance and Free
Advertising." Library of Congress, March 2016. https://
www.loc.gov/law/help/campaign-finance-regulation/
comparative.php.

Liptak, Adam. "Supreme Court Vacates Ex-Virginia Governor's Graft Conviction." *New York Times*, June 27, 2016. https://www.nytimes.com/2016/06/28/us/politics/supreme-court-bob-mcdonnell-virginia.html.

Narayanswamy, Anu, Darla Cameron, and Matea Gold. "How Much Money Is Behind Each Campaign?" *Washington Post*, February 1, 2018. https://www.washingtonpost.com/graphics/politics/2016-election/campaign-finance.

Norton, Ben. "1,240 Arrested in Past Week As 'Democracy Spring' Movement Against Money in Politics Spreads Throughout US." *Salon,* April 20, 2016. https://www.salon.com/2016/04/20/1240_arrested_in_past_week_as_democracy_spring_movement_against_money_in_politics_spreads_throughout_u_s.

Perdomo, Catalina, and Catalina Uribe Burcher. "Money, Influence, Corruption, and Capture: Can Democracy Be Protected?" In *The Global State of Democracy 2017: Exploring Democracy's Resilience*, edited by Kelley Friel, 124–156. Stockholm, Sweden: IDEA, 2017.

Rodd, Scott. "Lobbyist Gift-Giving at Issue in More States." Pew Charitable Trusts, July 19, 2017. https://www.pewtrusts.org/en/research-and-analysis/blogs/stateline/2017/07/19/lobbyist-gift-giving-at-issue-in-more-states.

Sang-Hun, Choe. "Park Geun-hye, Ex-South-Korean Leader, Gets 25 Years in Prison." *New York Times*, August 24, 2018. https://www.nytimes.com/2018/08/24/world/asia/park-geun-hye-sentenced-south-korea.html.

INDEX

Page numbers in **boldface**
refer to images.

ABOUT THE AUTHOR

Derek Miller is a writer and educator from Salisbury, Maryland. He is the author of more than a dozen books for middle school and high school students, including *Dilemmas in Democracy: Military Force* and *Dilemmas in Democracy: Voter Disenfranchisement*. In his free time, Miller enjoys reading and traveling with his wife.